Analog Journals
@Trio House Press

This journal is one of a series featuring the artwork of Jeffrey Scherer. Jeff is an artist living in Portland, Oregon. After working in Germany, France, and the United Kingdom, he co-founded Meyer, Scherer & Rockcastle, Ltd Architects in 1981 in Minneapolis, Minnesota, now called MSR Design.

He retired in the fall of 2016. For over 40 years his architectural interest and personal passion was the public library and its role in education. His work is concerned with the natural world and human condition. He uses his art work to help libraries and other not-for-profit organizations do more in their communities by giving his work for free in exchange for a charitable donation. All proceeds from the sale of this journal go towards funding the non-profit Trio House Press' mission of producing quality poetry and creative non-fiction titles.

If you would like to view or obtain one of Jeffrey Scherer's artworks, visit his website https://www.schererworks.com/

To view Trio House Press' other Analog journals, poetry books, creative nonfiction books, and more, go to our website: https://www.triohousepress.org

This journal cover features the painting _Grove at Sunset_ by Jeffrey Scherer.

I0389279

ISBN:978-1-949487-28-2

©2023 Trio House Press
2615 Emerson Avenue South
Minneapolis, Minnesota 55408
triohousepress@gmail.com